NOSTALGIA IN VERSE:

A COLLECTION OF POEMS AND SHORT STORIES FROM THE TURN OF THE CENTURY

Alexander Berberich

Copyright © 2023 by Alexander Berberich

All rights reserved.

ISBN 978-1-62806-373-8 (print | paperback)

Library of Congress Control Number 2023906089

Published by Salt Water Media
29 Broad Street, Suite 104
Berlin, MD 21811
www.saltwatermedia.com

Cover photo by the author
Author photo by Mmekutmfon "Mfon" Essien

NOSTALGIA IN VERSE

Dear Dad,

I am ok.

Love and miss you dearly.
Alex

CONTENTS

When I Went To Sleep 12
The Bus 14
Mon Amour 15
Love 16
A Look From Afar 17
It 18
Accordion 19
Wealth 20
My Life 21
Abigail 22
Loyalty 23
Please Understand 24
Not a Quitter 25
Canal Street 26
My Soulmate 27
Nica 28
Clear To Me 30
Demons 31
The Journey 32
The Prayer 33
Memory or Real 34
Tomorrow 35
This Life 36
The Church Bell 37
The Street 38
Light or Night? 39
Destiny 40
The Payphone 41
Up the Mountain 42
The World Pass By... 43

Life	44
Sleep	45
A Question of Morality	46
Accomplished	47
41 Bullets	48
An Unmade Bed	49
The Bee	50
Latin America	52
W.W.W.W.H.W.	53
My Innermost Fear	54
Why Beg?	55
The Walls	56
The Spot	57
Family	58
Desearía	59
What I Am Here For?	61
With Me or Against Me?	62
Bella	63
To Be Free	64
"Others"	65
The Plaza	66
Walking On a Line	67
The Bedouin	68
Friends	69
Mistake	70
The Saddest and the Maddest	71
The Concierge	72
Eternity	73
My Love	74
The Floridita	75
Peace	77
A New Me	78
The Circle	79

NOSTALGIA IN VERSE

Poems and Short Stories

WHEN I WENT TO SLEEP

One night I went to sleep, hot and sick to my brain,
When I woke, I was cold and felt no more pain.
I opened my eyes, to find myself lying in a driveway,
And though I went to bed at night, it never became day.
In front of me was a gate, too massive to ever climb,
With a sign in block letters that read "Next in Line".
Behind me was a driveway, twisting off into the darkness,
No way would I walk that, even with flashlights and partners.
There in that driveway, with dark clouds overhead,
I began to cry, wishing I was dead.
To my left and right seemed to be a wall that went on forever,
My body began shaking, my mouth tasted like leather.
I ran to the gate and pulled on it hard,
My body felt warm, but from entering I was barred.
Though touching the door made me feel sheltered, something I now began to hear,
Screaming and voices, so I had to let go to cover my ears.
I was now cold and began to cry again, feeling more and more alone,
In the distance there raised a dark and steady drone.
From behind I could hear the drone getting closer,
Slowly I turned and looked over my shoulder.
There I stood, frozen in place,
This is when I realized I was before heaven's gate.
What was approaching were thousands of souls that were straight pure evil,
I began to wonder how I became one of those people.
I fell shaking and crying to the ground, hoping it was all a dream,
It got colder and I realized the drone was really a scream.
The scream was coming from deep within my soul,
Messing with my mind, it was beginning to take its toll.

The darkness finally reached me, and began pulling me away from the gate,
At this point I felt nothing, just emptiness and hate.
As my cold lifeless body was pulled away to eternal time,
A bright light shined through the gate, which opened, and I heard "next in line".

THE BUS

The other night I dreamt of a bus filled with people,
Laughing and talking, all of us were equal.
Everyone was sharing food and thoughts like we were family,
I felt a new feeling burst up inside me.
Hearing all sorts of memories, and experiences not yet made,
The bus pulsed, alive with energy, but from its course never strayed.
In the flutter of a blink, everything was quiet,
No more talks about children, books or diet.
It was depressing, as if the bus was full of dead,
Waiting for the bus to stop, so all could spread.
What was I thinking, a dream is not real,
In my dream I was the driver, in control of the wheel.
I miss that bus, so full of life,
I wish I could drive it, off into the night.

MON AMOUR

My love,

I know you won't believe it, but it pains me to write this letter. I know I will hurt you, but I just cannot continue like this. You are a beautiful person, and you deserve so much better than me. You deserve to be with someone as generous and sensitive as yourself and above all as passionate. I am lost, and I do not want to hurt you anymore than I already have. I thank you for all the beautiful times we've shared. Those memories will remain with me always. Whenever I am lonely, I will close my eyes and remember all those beautiful moments. I wish I could love you with the same passion, but I can not. I pray that one day you find someone as special and wonderful as you. You will forever be in my heart, and I will always love you.

Ana

LOVE

Will I ever be in love?
Will I ever be loved?
Will there be a time that I can look in another's love-filled eye?
Will I see this moment while I am still young?
Will I see her before I am done?
Will I return the love long lost?
Will I be picky and see through it?
Will I be attentive and gravitate to it?
Will I be me, and she see it?
Will I be not, and she love it?
Will there be a day when I can commit?
Will there be a day from writing these poems I can quit?

A LOOK FROM AFAR

I recently took a step back and looked at my life from afar,
Attempting to see if emotions really leave a scar.
Looking over the great plains of life, at my personal account,
I saw familiar faces, wandering free and about.
I witnessed many people fall, and others help them up,
Bonding together and drinking from the same cup.
I was amazed how many people I thought were down for good,
Instead coming back stronger, as they knew they would.
Amid all the confusion, I forgot what I was here for,
To see how I faired with emotions, be it for good or for poor.
Amongst all the people, I couldn't find me,
So, I decided to look from atop a lonely tree.
From there I searched, around and around,
Looking over the landscape, both up and down.
I was about to give up when something caught my attention,
A man in a hole digging, eyes filled with tension.
The man digging was me, and the hole my emotional scar,
Looking back, I really wish I hadn't looked from afar.

IT

Why do I get lost and confused,
Striving for success while my ego gets bruised.
I crave it, desire it, yet fear it,
Trying, trying so hard just to achieve it.
When I get it, will I be content or greedy for more,
Or will I die without it, lonely and poor.
I must follow my heart and listen to what my conscious will say,
For now, I must get up and take it day by day.

ACCORDION

The old man with the accordion at the bus stop seemed to have no idea how much he sucked. Day after day, I would watch him try to collect change from passersby. Day after day, despite how hard he tried, I watched as hundreds of people ignored him. It struck me as odd that a man would go out there and play tuneless, off-key music for hours without receiving so much as a pittance for his effort. Doing such a thing every day - the man's tenacity amazed me. I began to wonder what drove him to be out there at that bus stop every day. Surely, it was not for the money, as he never made any. One day, during the intermission of one of his dreadful performances, I approached him and asked. Pushing his big bushy eyebrows skyward, he looked at me with a smile and said, "I know I'm awful, but I sure do like to play, son". From that day on, I've never enjoyed the sound of an accordion more than when I was at that bus stop.

WEALTH

Night after night and day after day,
I stress myself in so many ways.
Things I could have done, things I should do,
All the while my mind plays the fool.
Bury myself in misery so deep,
I can't even escape it when I am asleep.
Found my way in, know the way out,
Yet I don't do a thing but pout.
Am I special? – Am I unique?
Talk of wishful thinking is all my mouth leaks.
Can I step back and live in the present?
I think of tomorrow but do nothing to get it.
So many things in this world make my heart ache,
I feel like I cannot handle one bit of the weight.
I think I will close my eyes and try to escape the pain.
In my mind, it seems I have nothing to gain.
If we speak tomorrow, then I have not given in,
Keep in mind this does not constitute a win.
I feel I am worthless, so who would benefit?
If I could just do something to feel alive…. then I think I would not want to die.

MY LIFE

On the last leg of my journey, my thoughts begin to roam,
Thinking of all I have left, way back home.
Is it the same without me there,
Or does it exist in my mind's lair?
Will I be safe and return home unscathed,
Or will I be mourned, thought of as brave?
Brave for taking a chance and trying to experience life?
Brave it is not…that is supposed to be my life.

ABIGAIL

I think of her often, even now. Is she okay? Where is she? Does she know that someone out there loves her? So many miles and so much time separate us. I remember our time together well. How I wish I could get it back. Just to savor it again for a few brief moments would be worth everything I have. Abigail. Just as quickly as you entered my life, you left it. Why? It just doesn't seem fair. How I wish I could take care of you forever. You would always feel loved and safe. You would never have to worry about the things you have to worry about now. I would cherish your life and take all the pain away. It hurts right now, Abigail. It hurts to know that you are out there, and you need me. That you need anyone, and yet I cannot help. Amazing that the twenty minutes we spent together could have such a profound effect on my life. Though I don't know what has become of you, I do know that you have forever changed the way I think. Innocent, beautiful and sweet. How could you know the world would be so cruel? I should have snatched you up when I had the chance. At only six years old, I could have made the sour memories disappear and given you a brand-new life. Life without poverty, hunger and disease. Your hair should not be blonde from malnutrition, it should be as dark and beautiful as your skin. For the rest of my life, I will try to teach all that I have learned from you. Though I wish I could have brought you with me, your teachings will be the legacy I leave behind. Even as I sit and ponder why, I know you are touching the lives of many that seek knowledge. A gift you were given, as if you are an angel among us. That is why our time was so brief. That is why you were at peace, while I was dying inside. You know your place in this world, and you accept it. As my truck pulled out of your village and into the African sun, I looked behind and I saw you staring. What lay behind me was a life lesson learned. What lay ahead of me was a life experience I had to share. To this day, I still feel the sting of the tear rolling down my cheek.

LOYALTY

I wander through life, content but alone,
Feelings of attachment, I am often prone.
At the end of the day, I'm still alone.
It is rare to meet a person like you,
One that makes me feel happy, not sad and blue.
Grateful I am that you are in my life,
I will cherish this experience, both day and night.
Though I am not quite sure where this is going,
Not being sure is what keeps me from knowing.
I hope you remain a presence in my life,
No matter what the price.
I am a strange bird, it is often thought,
But a more loyal person you could find not.

PLEASE UNDERSTAND

Often, I wish for my own death,
Praying each time I breathe that it may be my last breath.
I am not sure why my thoughts can be so dark,
If not dead, why not a bird in the park?
If I were that bird, money would not be a pain,
As it stands now, my existence…money is the bane.
If I were that bird, I would just eat and fly,
Not have to worry about anyone, just me, myself and I.
There are many reasons that I am not happy with life,
Spend some time in my mind and you will understand my strife.
I am now wondering how the bird can survive,
No love, no feelings, just being alive.
Maybe I am better off with my own mental laments,
And until I do die, I will just remain tense.

NOT A QUITTER

Sometimes I want to quit, just give up,
I realize then, I would be stuck in a rut.
But would it relieve all the stress that keeps me awake?
I think it would bring me farther from my own fate.
Quitting is for losers, that I know I'm not,
Scared I do get, but the fear won't get me got.
The pressure gets to me, and I feel lost and alone,
I'm okay for now, when I'm not, I'll just write another poem.

CANAL STREET

This can't be happening. A few moments ago, I was going about my routine. Walking the same route that I have walked every day for the past 45 years. Suddenly, and without reason, I fell flat on my face. While a few stopped to assist, I saw others pass by looking down upon me as if I were an old car that wouldn't start anymore and shaking their heads as if to suggest that it was time to get rid of me. I open my mouth, but no words exit. It feels as though it were yesterday when I was bounding down this exact same street with my little ones at my side. My little ones… my life… all of it gone. Evaporated in front of my eyes. If I could just go back. Who is rubbing my back? A kind woman looks like she is trying to console me. My face hurts…numb. Another woman hands me a cup of ice and guides it to the side of my face. I want to go back to an earlier time.

MY SOULMATE

Although it is surrounded by flesh and bone,
My heart feels as if it is alone.
Will there be a day when it will be warm and coupled,
Or will it forever remain cold and buckled?
The days pass and I am not getting any younger,
With each day that passes, my heart moves closer to hunger.
Why – cannot I meet my soulmate,
Is alone and bitter to be my fate?
All I want is someone I can laugh, cry and share with,
Are these feelings too much to ask to die with?
If you are out there, my love, please be patient,
I am searching for you but am stuck in the basement.
I hid my heart down here some time ago,
I am trying to find it, but this I cannot forgo,
For me to find you and come up the stairs,
I need to be me, and my heart makes me care.
Once I find it, I will be on my way,
Just make sure from the basement you stay away.

NICA

Evelyn Elizabeth, a beautifully vibrant Nicaraguan girl of about 18. With two children, the weight of the world was on her young shoulders. She carried it well. I would start my mornings at the bakery she worked at to purchase a sweet bread and juice. Most of the time I would throw the sweet bread out, as I have never been much of a breakfast person. I just needed a reason to stop there. I would wake up and think that soon I would be peering into the deep, doleful eyes of a beautiful young woman. Playing her part, she would indulge my morning flirts and feed my ego. Underneath all that playful flirting lay a beautiful relationship that was slumbering, for the language barrier prevented any possibilities of truly getting to know each other. It was therefore an even more beautiful relationship in that there was not much more we could do but stare and smile at each other. Once I left the country, I would often romanticize our relationship in my mind. It had altered into a true love. A love that at times I truly felt existed. Time passes, heart breaks, heals, and then breaks again. The never-ending cycle of my existence up until that point. This made the fantasy that much more worthwhile to hold on to, in some chasm of my soul. The uniform of the bakery was such that it allowed little for the imagination. Every curve of her body, from the firmness of her breasts to the dimples in her lower back could be made out beyond the skimpy uniform. But it was her eyes. It was all about her eyes. The pain, the struggle, the strength. They were a window into her soul, and they were unforgiving in their story. We need not have been able to communicate, as I already knew it all. I felt the pain and I related. During my one year there, only once did I ever see her outside of the bakery. I was strolling down Avenida Central to catch a bus when I felt a caring touch on my left elbow. With the sun in my face, I turned and squinted only to be brought out of the haze of glare by those eyes. She was before me, no longer wearing her hairnet. Her jet-black hair was flowing freely as if it had been set free from the chains that kept her eyes enslaved. It was a moment that will forever be frozen in my mind as what life is. Life is about beauty and those unflinching moments of pure happiness that make all the bad stuff seem to just go away for an awkwardly long but nevertheless brief moment of time. Evelyn Elizabeth, how I wish I could go back to that moment and take away the pain. How I wish I could have saved you from your burden. Such a special person in such a cruel world. Billions of human experiences, so why does yours have to be so harsh? Why does the world make you feel useless and cheap? Questions that aren't important, but still, I want to try to understand. I wish I could impress upon you just how much it pained me to see you working as a prostitute. Never has my heart leapt, as when I discovered this. Such a special thing, and yet you believe that is all that is left for you to do to provide for your children. A pity. As I was sipping my drink and surveying the sea of women for sale, through the smoke and darkness I saw those eyes. Those eyes that now told an even deeper story. Eyes that know the consequences of your actions but are not allowing it to register in your brain. The windows to your soul have become so foggy that they have blinded you. I can think of no sadder moment than when I walked up to you. Those windows became clear, and the recognition came. The recognition of a time that, although difficult, was still somehow pure. There we stood, squished in between dozens of whore mongers negotiating their decadence, and we shared. We shared with our eyes all the pain we were both feeling at that moment, and then you wept. You apologized and wept. I drew you close, as if we had been lovers before, and I hugged you for the first time. I held you close, and you wept on my shoulder as the debauchery swirled around us. I said more to you with that hug than I have ever expressed to anyone in my entire life. I expressed my anger, my compassion, my support, my pain and my love with that hug. I looked into your soul one last time and kissed your cheek goodbye.

CLEAR TO ME

Day by day, I sit and pray,
For my life in this world to end one day.
To take all the pain and misery I see,
And have it become somehow clear to me.
People who hate, people who kill,
People who steal so they can feed their kids a solid meal.
Who is right?
Who is wrong?
Who am I to judge them all?
Once I die, I hope I can see,
And have it become somehow clear to me.

DEMONS

When I go to sleep, I'm not alone,
In my head, these Demons roam.
Roam and roam, all through the night,
It's as if each Demon had its own little plight.
A plight to remind me at all cost,
The Demons I thought I had lost.
I have no excuse for the actions I've taken,
But wish I could get through the night without shaking.
But the shaking is there, what do I do?
I created these Demons, and I must die with them too.

THE JOURNEY

Everyday I feel like I'm approaching death,
Straining to hold on to each little breath.
Filling my lungs with sweet smelling air,
Pondering why, we can't die as a pair.
To make the journey to the unknown with someone beside me,
A friend, a lover or just someone to guide me.
A guide would be nice, since I've had such a difficult time,
Choosing the correct path in this lifetime.
This would be nice, but a guide there will be none,
I must be strong, take my last breath, and accept that my time in this life is done.

THE PRAYER

The sun rising in the early morning sky, bringing with it the heat that would consume the day. The smell inside the taxi was musty yet pleasant. Arabic music came softly from the rear speakers. In limited English, my driver asked permission to stop and pray. Had it been anywhere else in the world, I may have said no. I had waited a lifetime to get here, a few more minutes would not hurt. The driver pulled over to the side of the road where a few dozen other men were gathered. The driver invited me to pray with him. Not being Muslim, I gently declined, saying I would not wish to disrespect his religion. He offered me his hand and said it was okay. It was his wish for me to pray with him. He grabbed a bottle of water from the trunk, and we set off in the direction of the gathering. As we approached the men, who all had their faces to the floor, the driver removed his sandals and requested I do the same. With the bottle of water, we washed our feet, hands, and elbows. This was the last of our communication for the remainder of the prayer. I followed him into a line behind other men. We stood shoulder to shoulder, toe to toe and began to pray. Standing, kneeling, bowing to the floor and standing again. Their chanting was soothing, and I began to relax. I found the praying to be peaceful. Soon we were done, and I was surrounded by men who wished to shake my hand and hug me. They thanked me for joining them in their prayer and wished me safe travels. As I turned to return to the car, the sun nearly risen, lay the great pyramids. They stood towering over the land. My entire life had been about getting here. My driver, sensing the personal moment, patted me on the back and allowed me to stand there and cry.

MEMORY OR REAL

Is my life a memory, or is it real?
Are my experiences my own, or did I steal?
Where could I get them…from another?
My teacher, my friend…or was it my brother?
I can't seem to remember what took place,
Is the memory I just made now on another face?
I wish I knew what really existed,
Memory gone…real obscured…my mind twisted.
I feel caught in the middle, in a state of flux,
My mind recalls peace…I guess I'm out of luck.
From where in my mind did that memory just come,
Or did it happen for real?… I'm fucking done.

TOMORROW

Today I sit here, lost and bemused,
Thinking about how much I'm confused.
Who do I trust, and who do I not,
I find myself sitting here, creating a plot.
People undermining me, trying to make me lose,
I'll be 101, and still putting in dues.
Why do I think about a plot when I should be at my peak,
Instead making me nervous and mentally weak.
I maintain a good attitude while giving 150%,
Other people gain and laugh at me sleeping in a tent.
When will everyone stop shitting on me, and give me my due turn,
One day to be happy, my dream come true, no more burn.
For now, those dreams, from other people I'll have to borrow,
And pray when I wake, my day will be tomorrow.

THIS LIFE

I'm alone with my thoughts, sitting in the dark,
Waiting for a noise, the phone, a knock, or just a bark.
Nothing is happening, but my brain keeps moving faster,
Catching a thought, I can't, I guess it didn't matter.
So many thoughts, racing through my mind,
I wish to be distracted, but for even a moment of time.
Distraction there is none, my head's working harder,
Telling me what I must do, no room for barter.
Disillusioned I'm not, as to the goals I must complete,
Knowing what's ahead of me is a tremendous feat.
During my mission, I shall lose many friends,
At the same time create enemies, do I care? that depends.
To get my goals accomplished, then care I will not,
To fail would just put me with the rest of the lot.
Failure is not an option, as you the reader can see,
This life is for the world, the next life can be for me.

THE CHURCH BELL

Why the church bell is ringing incessantly at 4:32 this morning, I have no idea. The bells have awakened me and brought me close enough to consciousness to become aware of the pressure building in my bladder. I rise from my bed and stumble to the bathroom. Having relieved myself, I peer from window to window, seeking the source of the church-bell clamor. I see but one lonely stroller. He seems a bit drunk or lost, or possibly a little of both. I return to my bed puzzled by the bells. Fully awake at this point, I find the constant ringing makes me angry – I need to sleep. Though I am not quite sure why this is going on, I'm quite aware of its effect on my night's sleep. An hour and a half later when the sun is beginning to rise, I still lay awake in my bed, listening to those damn bells.

THE STREET

Walking down a dark, desolate street,
Feeling nothing but the blood rushing through my veins, my heartbeat.
My eyes are open wide, and my ears tuned tight,
Searching and hoping for some sign of life, it's going to be a long night.
Every step, soft and precise, like a choreographed ballet,
So much on my mind, I open my mouth, yet I have nothing to say.
All I want to do is stop and catch my breath,
But every time I do, all I see is visions of death.
I can't turn around, as it seems I'm already lost,
Forced to keep going down the street, pushed around or bossed.
Occasionally, I try to get a glimpse over my shoulder,
Each time I try, my body gets colder and colder.
I hope soon the end of the street will come,
Then I'll be rid of this curse, set free, sprung.

LIGHT OR NIGHT?

God, I feel deeply that You exist,
Yet at times, it seems that I persist.
To doubt You, and all Your revelations,
To do what I know is wrong and dabble with temptations.
Living life so fast, sometimes it's hard to see,
The presence of the Devil, lurking around me.
See him not, but feel him I do,
Trying to enlist me, into his crew.
The pressure is strong, like my head under water,
A cloud rolling over, roaring with thunder.
Resist the pressure, resist the strain,
If I give in, only the Devil will gain.
It's hard to stay ahead, in a game I didn't create,
Each decision bringing me closer to my own fate.
In the end, will You free me, laying upon me Your light,
Or will the Devil's cloak of evil consume me in the night?

DESTINY

With so many choices, it's hard to choose,
Which decisions to make. One to win. One to lose.
Although I know my destiny, at times it is hard to define,
The foolish from the smart, they all rattle my mind.
They can depress me and motivate me at the same time,
I sometimes spend days like this, trapped in my own mind.
So whichever decision I make, all I can do is make the best,
Because in the end I know my destiny, bring it to me and put me to the test.

THE PAYPHONE

As I hung up the payphone, I came to the realization that it was the last time I would ever hear her voice. At that moment the world slowed to a deafening pace, crippling my senses. I slowly backed away from the bank of telephones and began searching for her. Surveying the scene, I saw old men sitting, children playing, people taking photos and couples kissing. My selfish perception was that they were all intentionally ignoring me, or was it my plight? I now began not to look for her, but for anybody. All I wanted was for someone to share a glance with me and understand, in that one look, all the pain that was shooting through my body. My eyes came to rest on a woman of about eighty. In the mass of humanity, she saw through me and everything I had experienced up to that point. She held my gaze for a few moments, then smiled. A smile of understanding. Warmth consumed my body and my heart felt as though it began to beat again. I returned the smile, wiped the moisture from my eyes and moved on before it started to rain.

UP THE MOUNTAIN

I sit alone on a mountain, dark clouds moving in,
Fresh air through my lungs, it's time to begin.
I close my eyes and rise slowly from the ground.
If I rise too fast, my head spins around.
I open my eyes and look at the valley below.
It's been a long journey, much taking its toll.
Now I am here, with memories to expound on,
I hope where I am going, they can also come.
It is time to continue my march up the mountain, with a weight lifting off me,
With each step I continue to die softly.
It is beginning to get darker, though I do not feel alone,
A humbling of the spirit and I stumble into the prone.
I lay down with my face in the soil,
Warmth consumes my body, my blood comes to a slow but steady boil.
My lungs deflate, exhausting all the air,
I wish this experience with someone I could share.

THE WORLD PASS BY...

As I sit here, watching the world pass by,
I wonder if I will complete all I want before I die.
Will I accomplish all my goals, take the giant leap,
Or will I fail and do nothing, if I do put me to sleep.
Save the world, I know I can't…
I take that back, not to try would only make me bland.
To make even the slightest impact, must change something,
Happiness or relief, to someone it must bring.
Now that I've spoken my mind, I'll leave you wondering why,
We'll see if you watch the world pass you by.

LIFE

The man with the olive complexion was dressed in expensive western clothes. He seemed a bit out of place in the open-air bazaar. As he sipped on his bottle of water, he meandered down one of the many aisles cluttered with small shops. I detected at least two bodyguards, that I could tell, following close behind. The man pointed at various objects throughout the marketplace that he wished to purchase. With each wave of his finger, people moved with excitement. It was not every day that the market saw such a wealthy individual. In his wake were personal assistants, struggling to keep up with paying for and carrying the purchases. Nearby was a man of about the same age. He was dressed in rags and filthy beyond belief. He approached the rich man and whispered something. The rich man bowed his head and offered the dirty man his bottle of water. The dirty man took a generous but not greedy sip from the bottle and returned it to the rich man. They then parted ways. Not long after, the rich man came close to me. I could not help but speak. I apologized for my ignorance, but I was curious about the whole exchange. The man took no offense to my question and calmly explained. This is the desert. In the desert, water represents life. It mattered not how dirty the other man was, nor how poor. If he requested a sip of water, he had no right to deny him, for denying him water would be denying him life. Such is the way of the desert.

SLEEP

Will I ever awake from this sleep,
Rise slowly, emerge from the deep.
Will I ever be able to see things change,
While asleep, all I can see is pain.
How can this be how it's supposed to be,
People living in misery.
I pray the world will awake from this dark deep,
Then my job will be over, and I can be put to sleep.

A QUESTION OF MORTALITY

At times I question my mortality,
Others tend to brush it off as a formality.
It is real, and something everyone must face,
That's why I put these people in their place.
Live your life as if you were to die today,
Don't be selfish, bitter or hateful, and you will be allowed to stay.
On this beautiful planet, with wonderful people,
Not to question mortality could become lethal.
For each sunrise I see, I acknowledge and pray,
Thank you for letting me see another day.

ACCOMPLISHED

As I sit writing this letter, I realize I have spent my whole life getting to this moment. Fifty-one years on this planet and here I am. As a young man, I longed for this day. I yearned to see all my dreams come to fruition. Back then, everything seemed so far out of my reach. For years I struggled and saved every penny. And now life cannot be more perfect. I have seen things that people have waited lifetimes to see and still have not experienced. I have created a totally unique life experience that most would be envious of. I have met all the goals I set out to achieve more than thirty-two years ago. I am healthy, financially secure, and proud of what I have done in this life. Therefore, at this moment, when everything is perfect, I must take my own life. It simply cannot get any better than this.

41 BULLETS

41 Bullets walking through the night,
41 Bullets itching for a fight.
41 Bullets, cold and dry,
41 Bullets looking to die.
41 Pulls of the trigger,
41 Bullets looking to get bigger.
41 Shots later they reached their goal,
41 Shots hitting an innocent man… taking their toll.

AN UNMADE BED

Somewhere in New York is an unmade bed,
A few hits of the snooze button and from bed they were led.
Through their morning routine without the slightest notion,
In a mere few hours, a new world would be in motion.
The two tall figures that were the backdrop to my life,
Exist no more, in their place, smoke from the fires clouding the light.
Their routine interrupted,
Life ceased.
Their beds left as they last lay in them…sheets in shambles, towers in ruin.
We are entering a new world that this time yesterday wasn't a thought,
We are now caught in the middle, and no one can be bought.
Good and evil are beginning to disappear,
Cause and effect have been brought up from the rear.
It will all be okay if I just close my eyes,
Picture the world yesterday – no, I can't lie.
We are in for a ride that will speed out of control,
I myself will be caught in it, taken for a stroll.
My routine broken, just another day,
Awoken from a bed that never got made.

THE BEE

My first experience with death was a traumatic one. Traumatic because I was five, and because I love honey. I was never afraid of bumble bees. I found them to be beautiful. The way they buzzed through the air with their black and yellow fur. They reminded me of a taxicab, with each flower they pollinated being another stop. And I love taxis as much as I love bees. I was always puzzled by people who became epileptic when a bee came near. To this day, I always think the bees are saying hello. They won't sting you unless they feel threatened. Swatting your hands, while bobbing and weaving uncontrollably, is a sure way to make a tiny life form feel threatened. I loved that this beautiful little creature could fly, kiss the flowers, and then produce the sweetest nectar. Nature. I would spend hours as a child watching them buzz around the garden. I would even name them and think they were my friends. It was mesmerizing. This was my world at the time. Sun, flowers, bees, and honey. Until the summer rain came. My mother placed me on the countertop next to the window so I could watch the world outside. There in the windowsill, next to dust and debris, lay one of my little friends. Completely still. I did not understand. I nudged him, but he did not move. It was at this moment, on a warm rainy summer afternoon in my fifth year of life that I became aware of the gross unfairness of death, and I began to cry. Especially when I realized he suffered, perhaps at the hands of me or my family. He most likely followed me into the home, became trapped, and then suffered a slow and miserable death trying to escape the home. This crushed me. Tormented me. I cradled the dead bee in my hands, and crying, brought him to my room. I placed him inside a ring box, with a piece of soft cotton. I prayed for him. The next day, I was still extremely sad. I brought the box with me out to the garden and went under the pine tree that was my hideout. I sat there, box in hand, crying. It all felt so unfair to me. I felt helpless. I dug a small hole, put my friend inside, and filled it back in. I placed a small white stone on top. From that day, until we moved, I would visit that site every day and apologize. I carried the burden of that bee's life with me until we moved from that home. Forty-five years later, I wonder what happened to that grave. I also wonder what happened to that boy.

LATIN AMERICA

The islands where I grew up in Greece are a distant but pleasant memory. They recall a time when life seemed pure and simple. When I was old enough, my father allowed me to leave home aboard a ship, a sailor. It was a proud day for both of us. I spent the next ten years sailing every ocean and sea of the world and visiting countries I had never heard of. I met people of different sizes and colors from cultures I never knew existed before. Once a year I would return home, my pockets full of money and my bags full of gifts. I would give the money to my father and the gifts to my younger sisters and brother. I was a Greek sailor, and my father was proud of his son. Now I am thirty-seven years old and living on the streets of a Latin American country whose name I can't even spell. I exist day to day on whatever I can acquire from begging. I find the American tourists most approachable. I show them the purple blotches on my legs, and they give me money to get out of their sight. I can't say that I am proud of this existence, but I, too, need to eat. I was thirty, and it was the first time I had visited the Philippines. There was a problem with Customs, so our departure was to be delayed by two days. I wanted to stay onboard and read. I felt as though I had seen everything I could of the port town. My shipmates convinced me otherwise. We spent much of the evening touring the local bars before we ended up at the brothel. It was the first time I had been with a prostitute. I remember that she was young, and possibly pretty, but beyond that I don't recall much. A year or so later we were stopped in Panama. All of us on the ship had to get visas to go to Russia, that is if we wanted to get off the ship. Part of the application required an HIV test. Two days later I found myself watching the ship on which I had spent the past ten years of my life and all of my shipmates sail off without me. I had a bag and a few hundred dollars. Since then, I have tried every day of my life to get back to the islands of my youth. Now, I must accept that I will not die near my family.

W.W.W.W.H.W.

WHO is going to kill me, this I cannot ask,
WHAT to kill me with, this is the killer's task.
WHEN I am to be killed, I can only hope for later,
WHERE doesn't matter, as I'll already be in danger.
HOW won't matter at this point, but I'd prefer to feel no pain,
WHY me, why now, is the last thing to go through my brain.

MY INNERMOST FEAR

I'm often in deep search, attempting to look and peer,
Into the depths of my mind, to find my innermost fear.
Amid each thought, idea, memory and dream, I creep,
Inspecting them all for the answer, while I'm awake or asleep.
I know the answer to this question, it haunts me day and night,
I strive not to think about it, avoid it, out of spite.
Living with a fear, I only hope never comes true,
Inquire all you want; you'll speak until your blue.
I made a pact with myself, the following is the deal,
My innermost fear, I shall never reveal.

WHY BEG?

As my face touches the cold concrete, I finally have a moment to pause and think about the events leading up to this moment. What could I have done to change the outcome? Of course, now, looking back, I see a dozen different things. All of that is bullshit now. The only thing that I need to be thinking about is how the fuck I am going to get out of this mess. As I open my mouth to try to convince these gentlemen that killing me would not be the best way out of this situation, a new thought crosses my mind. Do I really want to talk them out of it? It was merely twenty-four hours ago that I was wishing I was dead. Now? Now I am about to barter and beg for my life? Funny what a day does…well, a day and $200,000. That, after all, is why I had wanted to die in the first place. Being poor sucks. But then I hit it. The big one. $1,000,000 split five ways. With that kind of cash, I could have disappeared forever. Now, as the man places the muzzle of his gun to the base of my neck, I realize that without that money I am shit. Before I am able to tell him that I am not going to fight it, the gun explodes into my head, and everything goes black. Fucking money.

THE WALLS

The walls are closing in on all four sides,
It is only a matter of time before I die.
Should I scream out loud for help,
Or do I deal with the hand I was dealt?
I must be strong to go through this,
A few years earlier and it could exist.
Now I am older and getting down and down,
There never seems to be anything my way 'round.
I could scream for help, but something is in my throat,
It hurts to swallow, it hurts to cry,
But it hurts even more to know that the swallow is pride.

THE SPOT

In my head, there is a large dark stain,
It is beginning to cover most of my brain.
I know what the stain is, and stop it from growing I cannot,
Before long it will just be one giant spot.
I question whether I really want to stop it from growing,
For if I did, it might prevent me from knowing.
The spot is covering my ignorance, and allowing me to see the needy,
The spot lets me see clearly, but now I'm getting greedy.
Now I want, more and more, to help the human race,
I will do what I can and leave the spot in its place.

FAMILY

Why was I born with nothing but the best,
A loving family, food, and a place to rest.
What did I do to deserve such good care,
Parents and a brother who always were there.
Their support and love not once did waiver,
Even when I was stubborn and put them off 'till later.
Looking back on all the problems I thought I had,
I compare them to others and know I had it far from bad.
If I knew then what I know now,
My attitude wouldn't have gone up and down, like a bad day on the Dow.
But now is now, and then was then,
From all your love, I can change these mice to men.

DESEARÍA

I wish…
I wish…
I come here every day.
In the night.
In the day.
In the sun and in the rain.
I come here because you brought me here.
Our special place.
A place that holds the dearest of memories for me.
I come here to be closer to you.
I can feel you here.
Close to me.
I sometimes reach for the sky in a final attempt to touch you.
One last touch.
One last hug.
The pain is too great when I realize I can't.
Even though you flow through me, with each day, I feel more and more empty.
I come here to fill that void.
Alone.
Just me.
You.
And my wish.
You were always there for me.
Unconditional love and support.
Some days I expect to see you here.
But I only see you in my dreams and memories.
You taught me everything I know.
Everything I am.
You were the only one that understood me.
Without you, I am lost.

I miss you, father.
I told you a million time that I love you.
But not once did I tell you why I love you.
I love you for all that you were.
I love you for all that you sacrificed for me to be who I am.
I love you with all that I am.
I wish…
I wish you were here.
Here with me.

WHAT I AM HERE FOR?

I tend to wonder why I am here,
Is it for self-gratification, or just to peer.
Peer into the minds of these sad miserable people,
A state of mind that can truly be lethal.
It seems to me that everyone is so self-absorbed,
Wanting money, fame and riches, but mostly to be adored.
I sometimes slip, and think this way as well,
Then I observe those around me, and I would rather go to hell.
These people really kill me, because they just don't understand,
What it means to reach out and lend a helping hand.
Now, after some reflection, I know why I am here,
Not for self-gratification, and not to peer.

WITH ME OR AGAINST ME?

Are the people around me with me or against me?
Do they want to see me shine or wallow in misery?
Who do I love, who do I trust?
I have many goals to accomplish, it's victory or bust.
With an attitude like this, I can tend to be cold,
I act as though people with me are against me, so I am told.
This is how it may seem to others, but reasons there are many,
I never try to hide them; you can ask any.
Although I don't like being alone, it's what I must do,
Swallow my destiny whole while everyone else wants to chew.

BELLA

Life.
My life.
As a young woman I spent much of my time at the beach.
Thinking.
Reflecting.
Feeling.
Questions – the beach provided the answers.
Alone, but never lonely.
There is a warm presence that blankets my soul.
These moments remain with me.
It's as if nothing has changed.
So much has changed.
Looking back 60 years the sway of the sea is the same.
Surging with life.
The sun continues to set its glorious colors.
I have never stopped walking on that beach.
And now as I near the sunset of my life, I am grateful for my many experiences.
But long to be back in that moment, on that beach…in my youth.

TO BE FREE

These days I am finding it hard to find my place,
It seems I cannot even justify me in my own space.
For each time I think I fail,
It brings me closer from where I should prevail.
If only it were as simple as waiting to do and be,
I would have long ago completed the ideal "me".
This will not happen, nor should it,
I need to grab hold and just do it.

If there was one thing I wish I could be,
It would be to forever be free.
Free from all the pressure I feel,
Everyday is another one to steal.
Life is natural when not protected,
My body and my life feel disconnected.
I need then to be one in order to be free.
I just hope it happens before I leave.

"OTHERS"

Occasionally, I get depressed,
From all of this, added stress.
Why do I continue to give?
When all I really want to do is live.
It seems like I'm always climbing a wall,
And when I get to the other side, there's another that's more tall.
This I could deal with, if it was me by myself,
Instead, I have others, holding on for help.
All I can do is continue to struggle,
Up the next wall, loaded down with "others".

THE PLAZA

There was a rumbling in the distance. Moments later the sky opened. Hundreds of people scattered from the Plaza to seek shelter. I simply opened my umbrella and remained where I was. The only thing I wished to hide was my book, as I did not want it to be ruined. The rain became stronger, and the Plaza was now vacant. I felt no impulse to stir. I sat and watched immense raindrops hit the concrete with machine-gun-like velocity. The rhythm of the rain spray became therapeutic. I sat, lost in my own thoughts, isolated by the rain. The image of the once-crowded plaza, alive with people, had been washed away. All that remained were me and my thoughts.

WALKING ON A LINE

It seems like I am always walking on a line,
Straddling good and evil, praying for more time.
On the left is good, the right evil,
Staying on the line makes it seem equal.
I stray left, then bounce back to the right,
I always end up on the line, night after night.
The goal is to permanently go left,
I hope to accomplish this, sometime before my death.

THE BEDOUIN

Many years ago, when I was a young man, I would sit on a great stone looking out over the Gulf of Suez. This was a custom of mine, a routine if you will. Every day, at around four in the afternoon, I would walk the same path, to the same great stone and sit there until I felt that the time had come to move. I would sit there fascinated with what lay before me. The base of the Gulf of Suez, where it runs into the Red Sea, is a beautiful place. Stretching out into each direction on the horizon lay the coast of Saudi Arabia. Every day, while I had my routine, a little old Bedouin man had his. I would usually hear him approaching by the sound of his sandals crunching the sand beneath his feet. In the otherwise deafening silence, it was a welcome sound to hear my friend grow near. Our encounters were pretty much the same, day after day. He would approach, nod, and sit down next to me. There we would sit, sometimes for hours. We never spoke. From where I sat, I would study the man's profile. His skin was dark, with a leathery appearance. His face somewhat reminiscent of a sculpture, deep with wrinkles. The lines seemed to tell a story of his past. A past I often tried to visualize. His crow's feet were deep and thick around the eyes, yet he did not squint under the extreme light. All the wrinkles on the man's body seemed to lead to his eyes. For all the history that lay within his skin and time he had witnessed, his eyes looked no more than a day old. Sitting there, his breathing would grow so still that I sometimes feared he might have passed. Without warning, he would stand up. He would take one last glance out towards the horizon and then at me. He would look at me for a few moments, as if he were now studying me, then smile and move on. Once again, the silence would be broken with the crunching of his feet. I would watch him slowly meander off into the distance, on the path that ran along the rocky coast.

FRIENDS

Will my friends ever appreciate me, if so, when?
This is only fair as I've always been there till' the end.
Things are beginning to change, I can feel it in my heart,
Bones are in pain, brain hurts, I'm falling apart.
Will it take severed ties for them to realize what they had,
When they realize what I was it will be too late, so that makes me bad.
This I cannot let bother me, accomplish goals I must,
My friends tossed me to the side, violated the trust.
To die alone with no friends, with all my goals complete,
Is better to die with friends a failure, totally beat.
If I am wrong, I hope they will forgive me for my sins,
For now, I must move forward and see what tomorrow brings.

MISTAKE

As my body expelled every ounce of pleasure that it was able to produce, I opened my eyes and looked at the woman before me. Just as quickly as the feeling had mounted, it too had passed, and instead was replaced with a feeling of regret. In a moment of desperation and loneliness, I had let her charm get the better of me. Only moments earlier, it would have taken a gang of men to beat me off her (pun intended), but now, I want to be a thousand miles away. I tried to catch my breath, but to no avail, for now I was beginning to panic. What do I do, what can I say, to get out of her bed without further incident? No cuddling. I wish to disappear from this woman's life and forget that tonight ever happened. The pressure builds. I find myself unable to say a word, instead, lying down with her in my arms. As her breathing became heavier and she fell asleep on my chest, I lay awake waiting for tomorrow.

THE SADDEST AND THE MADDEST

The things in life that make me feel the saddest,
Are the exact same things that make me feel the maddest.
Like children who die before they have a chance to grow,
Or are gone before they become whole.
People who die because of a lack of food,
While others eat whenever they're in the mood.
Politicians who are worried only about their office,
Instead, they could be making changes, even if it meant their office.
People who murder and steal,
Unless it's for a just cause, they aren't keeping it real.
I thought writing this poem would help calm me down,
Instead, I must stop writing, as I feel like I'm about to drown.

THE CONCIERGE

'What if I were to tell you that I haven't stopped thinking of you since the last time I saw you…would you believe me?' The young beauty, startled but not fazed, answered back, 'I might.' What followed was silence. We locked eyes for several moments. The world buzzing around us came to a standstill. Blinking is what finally broke the spell. 'I'm afraid I don't know what to do now,' I said. Her gaze locked; she was just now coming to. 'What's your name?' she said. I felt trapped. Should I lie and escape, my pride still intact, or do I go for broke and stick around? 'Alex,' I said. 'Well, Alex, I'm afraid you are a touch too late.' A look of puzzlement must have fallen over my face. 'I see,' I said. With that, I turned and walked away, and through the revolving door that was the misery of my life. Maybe one day I will go back and find out what exactly I was too late for.

ETERNITY

Looking up, the moon was shining down bright upon us. The wind felt cool against my face. The body pressed against my back, holding on, felt warm. I maneuvered the motorcycle through traffic with the greatest of ease, the arms around my chest making me braver than I was. Her head rested on my shoulder, hair blowing in my face, carrying with it the sweet smell of honeysuckle. We must have driven around that island two dozen times, never wanting the night to end. The comfort and freedom we shared on that bike is unparalleled with any other experience in my life. She was my heart and soul, and that night we were one. So, as I lay here dying, and you ask me to recall a happier time in my life, that is what I think of. And should there be a heaven, I wish to be on that bike with her, riding around that island at night, for eternity.

MY LOVE

Every single day I think of you,
And all the things I want us to do.
Places to go, things to see and memories to make together,
To follow our hearts and remain one forever.
Our situation is hard, lots of times I feel like crying,
To say I don't think about you day and night would be lying.
We must stay strong for the time being,
Not waiver in our love, or our hearts will start bleeding.
Bleed our hearts won't, our love will become greater,
I think about you now and know I will still love you later.

THE FLORIDITA

I first saw her outside the Floridita, Hemingway's old haunt in Havana. As I exited the bar, I was taken back by the beauty of this woman. Our eyes locked for the briefest of moments, and she smiled a smile unlike any I had ever seen. She was tall, with beautiful dark skin and long flowing hair. Her face had the most remarkable structure, with a set of hazel eyes that could have melted a chocolate bar. I stood frozen in place, totally flabbergasted by the sight of this exquisite woman. The smell of the air that day forever lingers in my mind as one of beauty. Her purpose in front of the Floridita was to hand out fliers for a salsa band that was performing that night at a club in Old Havana. Just then she handed me one. Attempting to seize the moment, I mustered up the courage to speak with her. Her name was Manuela, and her sister was the lead singer of the band. She was twenty-one years old and her whole family would be there that night. Had she asked for anything in the world at that moment, I would have delivered it. I thanked her for the flier and said that maybe I would see her at the club. Her response was, "I hope so." As I walked away, I turned around one last time and saw that beautiful smile bidding me a wonderful day. After that, I was a bit lighter on my feet, desperately wanting to know more about her. I didn't want to sleep with this woman, I wanted to be with this woman. The moment I saw her I had a vision of my life with her, and it was beautiful. I spent the rest of the day walking around in a state of bliss. Whether she was even interested in me, I cared not. All that was important to me was that I would be able to look at her, and with luck get to know her as a person. I wanted to know her heart. That evening, I took an extra-long shower. Having slipped the maid some capitalist toothpaste, I was able to get the most immaculately ironed shirt I have ever worn. I departed the hotel early enough to walk off some of the butterflies in my stomach. It still being early, I was the first person to arrive that evening. The band was setting up in the courtyard of the old home that had been converted into a club. I took a seat where I would be able to survey the entire room and began my wait. With every motion I noticed from the door, my heart would flutter, only to be disappointed when others entered. I often wonder what would have happened, had she ever walked through those doors that evening.

PEACE

Will there ever be a time,
When I can rest, pure peace of mind?
So many things that question my fate,
Leaving me in an unbalanced state.
All I want is peace and happiness to endure,
Leaving ahead of us tasks that are quite a chore.
Sometimes I question my own train of thought.
My mind confused; soul torn apart.
If there is ever to be peace of mind,
I hope it lasts me until the end of time.

I often feel threatened by my intelligence.
Am I smart or dumb…or just a waste?
I tend to lean towards the latter,
Sometimes I feel like I could just shatter.
If there ever was a place to be at peace,
I haven't found it… but I've tried grinding my teeth.
Should I continue the search or just cave in?
I swear to God I feel like the devil is about to win.

A NEW ME

A new me is about to begin,
Leaving the world I associate with sin.
I am on a quest to find my soul,
If I do not find it, I will be in a hole.
Is it my soul that I am looking for,
Or is it to see what is behind the door?
The door that lays at the reach of my hand,
The door that leads me to become a man.

THE CIRCLE

The house made noises. Especially at night. The stairs creaked as if someone were walking on them. The clicking of the thermostat. A distinct sound followed moments later by the whoosh of air bellowing from deep within the basement. My father snoring in the next room, the dog having a bad dream. I close my eyes. I can hear it all. I can feel myself, in my bed. The streetlight glowing in above the half-window curtains, casting crisscross shadows onto the ceiling. Safe. That is how I felt. How many nights? How many nights like this did I take for granted. Thousands, I suppose. I close my eyes. I go back to one of those nights. I pick one, at random. I imagine myself flying over the house and get out of that bed…and walk through the house. It is all still there. We are all still there. What I would give to go back to one of those nights right now.

ABOUT THE AUTHOR

Alexander Berberich was born in New York City and is a filmmaker, event producer and boat captain. Known for his passion for travel and exploration, he has traveled to over 86 countries and 48 states.

www.alexanderberberich.com

Author photo by Mmekutmfon "Mfon" Essien circa 1997 in Harlem, NY.

www.ingramcontent.com/pod-product-compliance
Lightning Source LLC
Chambersburg PA
CBHW070758050426
42452CB00012B/2394